asking

looking

playing

making

tonkin.

first

david rock

word

this little book betrays its size
by explaining a big concept.

of designing in a different way.
of approaching the client's brief
uniquely. of discovering the creative
spark - that essentially differentiates
architecture from mere building -
by coming from a new direction.

a concept which can be applied,
and has been, to projects large
and small, to buildings and
interior design.

asking, looking, playing making
brings new meaning to those words.

this
book

here we propose a method for
developing concepts that are
specific to person, place and time.

asking, looking, playing, making is the
framework for our creative inquiry.
the goal is to originate concepts that
will stay true and be understood
through archetypal form. the hope
is for an architecture that is both
particular and accessible.

nine stories illustrate nine projects.
the range in scale and type demon-
strates the versatility of our method.

glow, grow, flow, float, our creed,
outlines the primal elements that
underpin our output.

asking

looking

playing

making

what is it?
what was it?
what could it be?

it is
it was
it could be

invent it
identify it
intensify it

convey it
control it
complete it

asking

why ask?
to find the story, and a new solution.

what to ask?
ask your instincts, what is the ideal?
forget the facts, first, what is the folklore?
get to the bare bones, go back to the beginning.

how to ask?
psychoanalyse your clients, what are their motives?
play the role of the man on the street, play the fung
shui master. search for freaks, assume nothing.

looking

why look?
to illustrate the story, to paint the words.

how to look?
see the chain of events. from the steel towers see
the steel rolling, through the mill, back to hills, into
the iron ore. see like you never looked, look like you
never saw, travel.

where to look?
rummage through your icons, you will find the collective
subconscious. study the trees that grow in the same
wood, what does history tell you. scan the new found
scales of nature. look through the microscope, look
through the mirror, look beyond the machine.

playing

why play?
a notion is just a feeling, an idea is just a part, a concept
is the whole. when a notion works, it becomes an idea.
when a series of ideas hang together, they form a
concept. when the concept works on many level, it
becomes a story.

how to play?
make psychological maps that take human senses
and place them in space. make typological maps that
leap — frog historical types. the final map is a diagram.
the diagram is the essence of the story.

who plays?
play with light, weight, colour, scale, time, and instincts.
start with the ordinary, invert expectations and make
the extraordinary. intensify by reduction and expand
with illusion. the final space will be a three dimensional
performance of the story.

making

why make it?
to tell the story.

who makes it?
use the help of someone who loves to build. control
the money and the time, and you control the quality.
limit the palette of materials, know them as friends,
know their sensuality and how far they can go.

how to make it?
use your common sense, be practical, keep the details
straightforward and the story will be easily told. the
best details are the ones that disappear. the whole is
more important than the parts, small is out, think big.

nine
stories

blood	broadway cinema
hill	edinburgh centre
cave	flex bar
castle	hugo house
maze	lane crawford store
forest	private i salon
time	q restaurant
jungle	tong zhi club
ruin	ubud hotel

broadway

in the first theatre
two men fought
blood was drawn

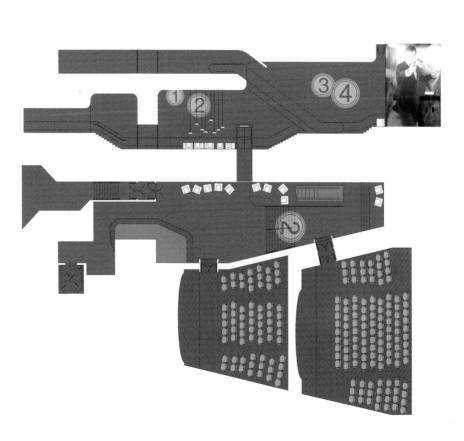

flock to the big screen
watch the killing

red is a thrill

red is power
red is new
red is second
only to white

edinburgh

edinburgh architecture and
design centre takes the form
of a glowing astro turf hill

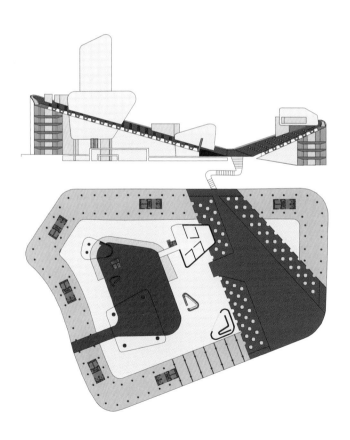

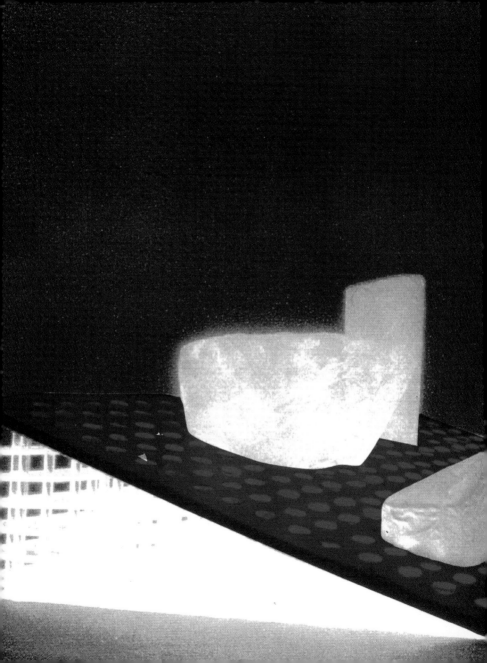

hill

plaza

boulders

cavern

park

flex

flex is a cave for men

men walk into
the mauve passage

men watch in
the big violet bar

men touch in the
small purple room

this is a fertile city

hugo house

a white castle to the sea.
a black castle to the road.
above its own beach, pinned
to the cliff by a red chimney

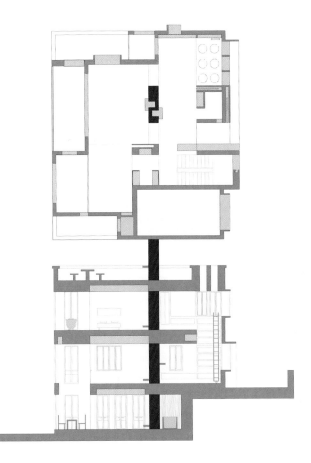

through thick walls

through thick ceilings

flows the sea breeze

lane
crawford

ladies fashion is a transparent maze.
a circuit on the floor guides your feet.
a circuit on the ceiling guides your eyes.

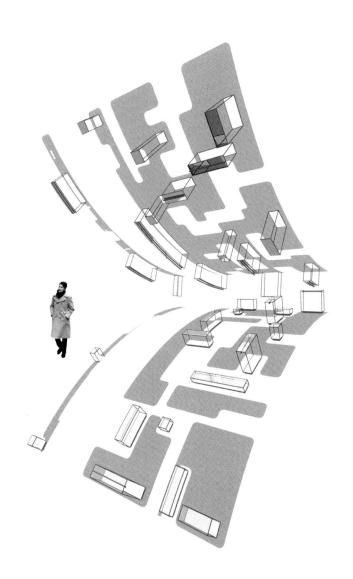

private

i

private i is a forest of hair that floats

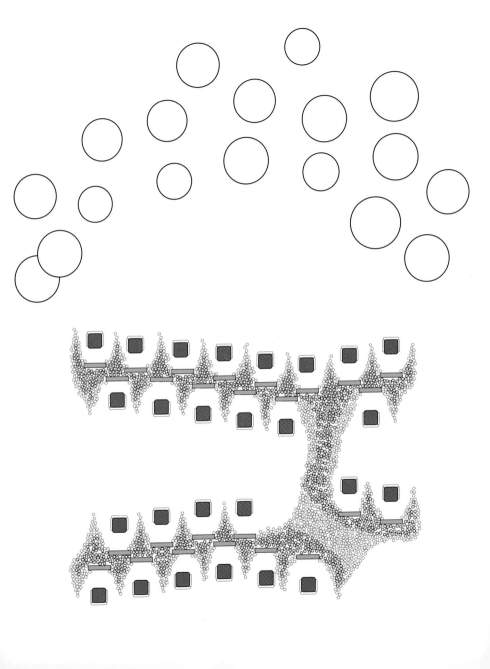

a trip to
the saloon
is a trip
into space

9

hong kong the flowing hills
slowly shaped by time

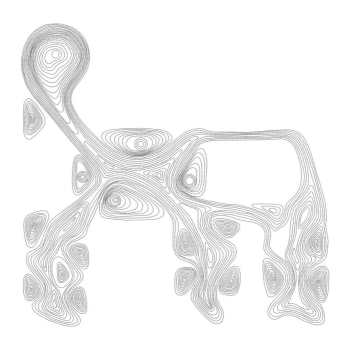

q the flowing ceiling saw to

wood for weeks

hong kong the neon city

a city faster than time

q
the neon sun
sunrise to
sunset in
half an hour

tong zhi

tong zhi takes karaoke from
the living room back to the jungle

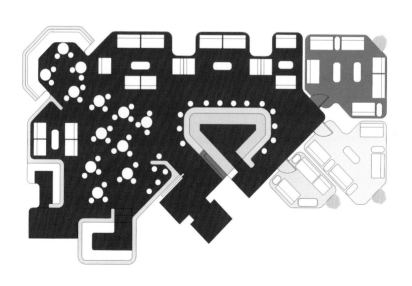

the leaf pattern
of wallpaper makes
us feel safe.
we used to sing
in the trees.

ubud hotel

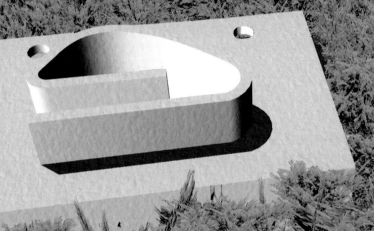

we walk in the hills
we look at the ruins
we go back to the water

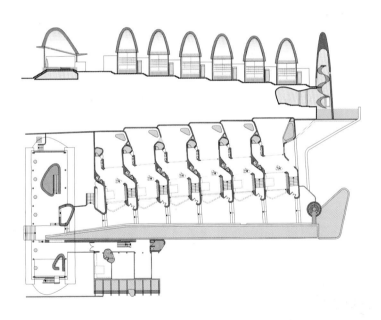

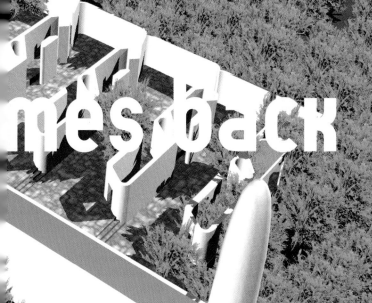

glow

grow

flow

float

glow is our primal
attraction to light

grow is the power
of nature over man

flow is the chi of
the physical world

float is the power
of man over nature

glow grow

glow	grow
animal	vegetable
fire	earth
orientate	shelter
light	life
daily	seasonal
nature's power	nature's renewal

flow   float

flow	float
mineral	artificial
water	air
move	space
time	freedom
constant	future
nature's cycle	nature defied

credits

instigated by paul archer
written by mike tonkin with anna liu

project graphics by hybrid*
david bothwell and alice lee

projects   year   ## photography

broadway*   1996   jonathan pile, mike tonkin
edinburgh*   1995   mike tonkin
flex*   1997   jonathan pile
hugo   1996-97   freeman wong, andrew wood
lane crawford   1996-97   jonathan pile, freeman wong
private i*   1997   red dog, mike tonkin
q   1994-95   jonathan pile, lily wang
tong zhi*   1996   freeman wong
ubud   1994   paul archer, mike tonkin

hong kong and london 1994-98

paul archer	jason hutchins	roy mak	gonzalo surroca
carolyn bemis	olivia hyde	dan morrish	colette tedden
rose bries	jeanette ko	benaim murray	mike tonkin
jim burkholder	simona lai	benjamin pan	nick tyson
ming wen chung	lewis lau	jonathan pile	helen tsoi
brian chan	carling lau	stephen power	giles vallis
bird choi	anna liu	bein kian saw	cindy wong
mike fisher	linda lu	taz shaikh	alana wilkins
wendy fong	fanny luk	helen sisley	lily wang
vicky fong	barra mac ruairi	daniel seyd	cyan yang
mathias frei	paul mcaneary	justin smith	gordon young
dan harris	tim mcdowell	yvonne stephens	clarie yung
richard harrison	jane mclennan	gregory stobbs	

colophon

all opinions expressed in material contained within this publication are
those of the authors and not necessarily those of the editor or publisher.

© 1998 black dog publishing limited and the authors
edited and produced by duncan mccorquodale
designed by christian küsters
typeface designed by herbert bayer (architype)
printed in the european union

isbn 1 901033 51 1

british library cataloguing-in-publication data. catalogue record for
this book is available from the british library. library of congress
cataloguing-in-publication data: asking, looking, playing, making, tonkin.

720/TON
N/L